1 MONTH OF FREE READING

at

www.ForgottenBooks.com

By purchasing this book you are eligible for one month membership to ForgottenBooks.com, giving you unlimited access to our entire collection of over 1,000,000 titles via our web site and mobile apps.

To claim your free month visit:

www.forgottenbooks.com/free919434

ISBN 978-0-266-98576-1
PIBN 10919434

STATE OF MICHIGAN

𝔇epartment of 𝔓ublic 𝔍nstruction

LANSING

THE
DUCATION OF HANDICAPPED
SCHOOL CHILDREN
IN MICHIGAN

BULLETIN NO 11

Published by
The Superintendent of Public Instruction
1926

STATE OF MICHIGAN

Department of Public Instruction

LANSING

THE EDUCATION OF HANDICAPPED SCHOOL CHILDREN IN MICHIGAN

By

CHARLES SCOTT BERRY

Professor of Educational Psychology, University of Michigan, and Director of Special Education, Detroit Public Schools

Bulletin No. 11

Published by
The Superintendent of Public Instruction
1926

CONTENTS

PREFACE

This bulletin is an attempt to direct the attention of superintendents and principals to the importance of making more adequate provision for the education of handicapped children, and at the same time to make helpful suggestions relative to the organization and administration of special classes for these children. Since the State of Michigan enacted legislation in 1923 providing adequate state aid for the education of the blind, deaf, and crippled in the public schools, there is now no good reason why these unfortunate children should not be given the care, training, and instruction best suited to their needs.

The writer wishes to express his indebtedness to the following persons for helpful suggestions in the preparation of this bulletin: Miss Alberta Chase, Secretary of the Michigan Society for Crippled Children, Ann Arbor; Miss Cordelia Creswell, Supervisor of Special Classes, Grand Rapids; Professor C. M. Elliott, Director of Special Education, Michigan State Normal College, Ypsilanti; Supt. I. B. Gilbert, Michigan School for the Deaf, Flint; Dr. H. A. Haynes, Superintendent of the University of Michigan Hospital, Ann Arbor; Supt. C. E. Holmes, Michigan School for the Blind, Lansing; and Miss Fanny Fletcher, Supervisor of Classes for the Blind and Partially Sighted; Miss Alice B. Metzner, Supervisor of Special Classes; Miss Clara Stoddard, Supervisor of Speech Improvement Classes; Miss Gertrude Van Adestine, Principal of the School for the Deaf; Miss Grace F. Woolfenden, Principal of the Nellie Leland School for Cripples, all of the Detroit public schools.

I. THE BLIND AND THE PARTIALLY SIGHTED

Investigations made in various parts of the country bring to light the fact that from 10 to 30 per cent of the school children have vision sufficiently imperfect to need medical attention. These investigations also show that long continued use of the eyes under unfavorable conditions results in impairment of vision. The lengthening of the school year and the period of compulsory school education, the increase in the reading of newspapers, and the remarkable patronage of the movies have greatly increased the demands made on the eyes. While it is true that much has been done to correct defects of vision and to improve the conditions under which the eyes are used, yet the needs of the children- most seriously defective in vision have not received adequate recognition in the public schools of our state.

From the educational point of view a blind child may be defined as one who cannot see well enough to be taught reading through vision but must learn by means of touch. The classes for such children found in the public school are known as "classes for the blind", or better "braille classes". In these classes they are taught to read by touch alone.

According to the United States Census there were in 1920 only 234 blind children in Michigan between the ages of 5 and 19, inclusive, and of this number 171 were enrolled in the Michigan School for the Blind. It is evident from these figures that outside of the largest two or three cities in the state there are not enough blind children to make it feasible or desirable to form special classes for them in the public schools. Provision has been made for their education and occupational training at state expense in the Michigan School for the Blind at Lansing which provides for their education from the kindergarten through the high school, and in the Michigan Employment Institution for the Blind at Saginaw, which furnishes occupational training for the blind who are between 18 and 60 years of age. However, neither the Michigan School for the Blind nor the Michigan Employment Institution are training schools for blind persons who are feebleminded. These should be sent to Lapeer, as the major defect determines the type of institution or school to which the individual should be sent. Much harm has been done to the cause of the education of the blind by failure to realize that blindness is in no way related to feeblemindedness.

The number of partially sighted children is many times greater than the number of the blind. A practical method of estimating the number

5

of such children that should be in special classes is to take the number actually found in these classes in the cities that have been most progressive in the education of the partially sighted. For it is hardly likely that any city has too many children in such classes. In one or more cities in Ohio the number of children in special classes for the partially sighted runs as high as one child for every two thousand general population. If the same ratio holds true in Michigan, there are about 1,800 children of vision so defective that they should be educated wholly or in part in special classes or in special schools. This means that in every city of ten thousand inhabitants or above there are probably enough partially sighted children for a class of at least five pupils, thereby coming under the law that provides state aid for the education of these children. (Appendix A). For it is now possible for the boards of education in these cities to educate the blind and partially sighted in special classes and receive state aid to the extent of the excess of the cost of the education of these children over the average cost of the education of children in the eight grades up to an amount not to exceed two hundred dollars per child. At the present time little special education is provided for the partially sighted outside of the largest two or three cities in the state although there are in Michigan twenty-eight cities of ten thousand inhabitants or more which comprise fifty-one per cent of the population of the entire state. The superintendents of these cities should realize that it is now possible to provide for the adequate education of the blind and partially sighted in special classes with no greater cost to the local community than if they were to remain in the regular grades.

First, let us consider the education of the partially sighted in cities large enough to have a special class before we take up the education of these pupils in the rural districts and in the smaller cities where there are not enough such children to form a special class. From the point of view of education, the partially sighted child is one whose vision, even after it has been corrected as far as possible by glasses, is so defective that he cannot read ordinary print at all or without injury to vision, yet is able to read large print. The classes that have been formed for such children in the public schools are commonly known as "conservation of vision classes" or "sight saving classes". The latter name is preferable.

In selecting pupils for a sight saving class there evidently is little difficulty in finding the child whose vision is so defective that he cannot even with glasses read ordinary print. The problem is to discover those pupils who are able to read print of ordinary size; yet in so doing are straining their eyes. Half the pupils in the sight saving classes of Cleveland are myopes.

Where there is regular medical inspection of all school children, those suffering from serious defects of vision will usually be discovered. However, such children should be given a careful examination by a competent oculist before they are placed in a sight saving class. Where there is no regular medical examination of school children, teachers can be quickly trained to test the vision of their pupils with sufficient accuracy to discover the more serious defects. In some states the teachers are required by law to test the vision of all school children. The teachers should refer all cases of seriously defective vision to the school physician and the cases he finds to be serious should be referred to a competent oculist for thorough examination, in order that the exact nature of the defect may be determined. Upon the recommendation of the oculist the child should be placed in the sight saving class. However, it is important that the oculist be fully informed in regard to the nature of the work done in a sight saving class, the size of print used, the lighting of the room, etc., in order that he may know what relief may be secured from eyestrain by placing a child in such a class. On the other hand, to get the best results, it is necessary that the teacher have from the oculist a written statement relative to the nature of the defect and its treatment, the extent to which the eyes may be used and under what conditions, and how frequently they should be re-examined. It is part of the work of the teacher to see that these instructions are faithfully carried out.

It is desirable to have a classroom of about standard size for the sight saving class. Although the enrollment in such a class seldom exceeds fifteen pupils the extra space is used to good advantage. Considerable room is required for the movable seats, the tables, typewriters, and cabinets that constitute part of the equipment of the sight saving room. The large room makes it possible for the pupils to move their seats nearer the windows on dark days. Furthermore, the necessary room is provided for the giving of simple exercises to relieve the eye strain which so quickly develops in most children with defective vision. Then again there are few school buildings that have small rooms well enough lighted for a sight saving class.

The location of the classroom in respect to lighting is very important. From the standpoint of general health as affecting the eyesight, a certain amount of direct sunlight is desirable. On the other hand it is imperative that the light be fairly uniform in intensity. The classroom that has a northeast exposure is thought to be the best in meeting these conditions. However, if the northeast exposure is not possible the order of preference is as follows: east, north and east, northwest, west, north and west, north. In order that a sufficient amount of light may be provided the area of the window glass should not be less than one-fifth that of the floor space.

The windows should be provided with window shades in order to control and diffuse the direct sunlight and to eliminate as far as possible glare from the blackboards. A satisfactory method of securing these results is to equip each window with two shades operated with double rollers placed near the middle rail of the window. Since the shades can be raised or lowered from the middle of the window, this arrangement permits the opening of the window from the top or bottom without moving the shades. Shades of a buff colored translucent material both diffuse and transmit the light. It is also desirable to have the walls light buff in color and the ceilings white or light cream, while the wood work should be of a dull finish and not too dark.

When sight saving classes were first started no artificial lighting was provided for; when the daylight was not sufficient, work was discontinued. However, so much time was lost that it became necessary to provide artificial lighting. The direct and semi-indirect systems of lighting are now in common use. For the average room with a floor space ranging from 720 to 900 square feet from four to six fixtures should be installed. From two and one-half to three watts per square foot of floor area should be provided with the indirect or semi-indirect fixtures.

Every sight saving room should be provided with an abundance of blackboard space as all writing must be large to avoid eyestrain. Movable desks and seats are necessary in order that the pupil may adjust his position to secure the right amount of light and to avoid glare. In addition the room should be provided with the following: A long table and the necessary chairs, as much handwork is undertaken in these rooms; a cupboard to hold the bulky supplies; a book closet for the large type books which are used only in the sight saving class; a typewriter and stand, as every partially sighted child should be taught typewriting; large sheets of rough manila paper and large lead pencils that make a broad black line; and the necessary supplies for handwork.

The number of pupils recommended for a sight saving class usually ranges from twelve to fifteen. However, some classes have less than twelve and other classes more than fifteen. The number that can be taught satisfactorily by one teacher depends on the range of grades represented and the character of the work attempted.

The subject-matter of instruction in sight saving classes is, generally speaking, that of the regular grades with more emphasis placed on the activities that can be carried on with minimum eye strain. Where this principle is carried out more attention is given to oral instruction and to oral learning. The aim is to give these children the type of training that will provide them with an education and at the same time teach them to care for their eyesight. The subject-matter is chiefly that of the regular grades since the partially sighted, as far as possible, recite with the seeing pupils in their regular grades, under the regular grade teachers. Furthermore they take the same examination the seeing pupils take, the examination questions being made out, not by the special teacher,

8

but by the regular grade teacher. This means that the partially sighted pupil is compelled to meet the requirements of the regular grade. The function of the special teacher is to assist the partially sighted child in the preparation of his work and to train him to conserve his vision as far as possible in all activities that involve the use of his eyes. In the teaching of arithmetic much more oral work than is the practice might well be given, for the arithmetic of every day life is chiefly oral. All writing should be done either on the typewriter, on the blackboard, or on manila paper. Too frequently the writing of both the teacher and pupils is too fine to be read without eyestrain. The pupils should be taught to rest their eyes after short intervals of work. One important object of the sight saving class is to form proper habits in the use of the eyes, which will function in the home as well as in the school. In order that this end may be attained the teacher should make frequent visits to the home to instruct the parents and enlist their active cooperation in the proper care of their child's eyesight. The stress should be placed on oral not on written composition as most of the partially sighted will necessarily enter occupations where little or no writing is required.

Skill in the use of the typewriter, a thorough knowledge of oral arithmetic, health and control of the body gained through proper exercise and training, and correct use of oral language may all be acquired without injury to the eyesight of the partially sighted child.

Since individual progress of the partially sighted is so closely bound up with individual instruction, it follows that the teacher should be one whose first interest is in the individual, who loves the individual in the concrete, not merely as a member of the group. She must be able to encourage those who have become disheartened through repeated failure. In addition to interest in the child and enthusiasm for the work, she must be characterized by resourcefulness and initiative for since she has greater freedom than the regular grade teacher she needs these qualities to use that freedom to best advantage. She must be able to get along well with others for it is necessary for her to work in the closest cooperation with the physician, with the home, and with the regular grade teachers in the school where her class is located. But in addition to the personal qualities mentioned the successful teacher of the partially sighted should have a certain type of training and experience. The best thought of the present time inclines in the direction of selecting teachers for the blind and partially sighted only from that group of teachers who have had successful experience in teaching seeing children. This seems wise since our aim is to prepare the blind and partially sighted children to live with normal seeing individuals.

Sight saving classes in the puplic schools have abundantly justified their existence. They have made it possible for many children to get an education who otherwise would have been denied the opportunity;

they have given to these children proper training and instruction in the care and use of their eyes; and they have stimulated the regular grade teachers to pay more attention to the eyesight of their own pupils.

But what shall be done for the partially sighted where there are not enough to form a special class is the problem that confronts the school officials in the smaller cities, towns, and rural districts of the state. Under the law providing state aid, these children may be sent to a district where there is a class for the partially sighted. Where this cannot be done they may be sent to the Michigan School for the Blind at Lansing, for this institution receives the partially sighted as well as the blind. But since the parents in most cases seriously object to sending a young child to the state school for the blind unless he is almost blind, it is necessary to make provision for his education in the regular public schools. This can be done to some extent at least, by seeing that the child is seated where he gets sufficient light of uniform intensity, by giving him careful instruction and training in how to care for his eyes, and in securing for him the most necessary of the large type books. In addition he should be provided with rough manila paper and heavy lead pencils for written work and should be taught as soon as possible to use the typewriter. Furthermore the parents should be instructed in how to care for the eyes of their child, for the work of the school cannot be very effective without the support of the home. If these simple suggestions are carried out many a child with seriously defective eyesight will be able to secure a public school education without further impairment of vision.

The first step for any superintendent to take who contemplates forming a special class for the partially sighted is to determine the number of children in his school who should be in such a class. He should read carefully the law given in Appendix A relative to the conditions under which state aid for such classes may be obtained. If its provisions are not clear, he should write to the superintendent of public instruction for an interpretation.

Cards for the testing of vision may be obtained from the C. H. Stoelting Company, Chicago, Illinois. Full instructions for the giving of tests of vision by teachers may be found in *Medical Inspection of Schools* by Gulick and Ayres, or in *Eyesight of School Children* by Berkowitz. Detailed information in regard to organization, equipment, and administration of sight saving classes is given in the *Manual for Conservation of Vision* by Winifred Hathaway. This manual should be in the hands of every superintendent who attempts to organize a sight saving class. The large type books for sight saving classes may be secured from the Clear Type Publishing Company, 2025 East 93 Street, Cleveland, Ohio.

It is not considered desirable to attempt to educate blind children in the same class with the partially sighted because the methods of

10

instruction are so different and because the blind child has a depressing effect on the partially sighted. As already stated where there are not enough blind children to form a special class it is better for them to attend the school for the blind at Lansing. If further information is desired in regard to the education of children who are blind, write to the superintendent of the Michigan School for the Blind, Lansing, or if it is a question of occupational training for the adult blind, write to the superintendent of the Michigan Employment Institution, Saginaw.

SELECTED REFERENCES

Berkowitz, J. H., *The Eyesight of School Children.* Bulletin, 1919, No. 65. Bureau of Education, Washington, D. C.

Best, Harry, *The Blind.* The Macmillan Company, New York, 1919

Gulick, L. H. and Ayres, L., *Medical Inspection of Schools.* Charities Publication Committee, New York, 1913

Hathaway, Winifred, *Manual for Conservation of Vision Classes.* National Committee for the Prevention of Blindness, 130 East Twenty-Second Street, New York, 1919

Irwin, R. B., *Sight-Saving Classes in the Public Schools.* Harvard University, Cambridge, Mass., 1920

II. THE DEAF AND HARD HEARING

Investigations that have been made indicate that from 10 to 20 per cent of the school children do not have normal hearing, and that the hearing of from 2 to 5 per cent is seriously impaired. But, it should be borne in mind that there must be an impairment of hearing amounting to almost 30 per cent before the subject experiences much difficulty in understanding ordinary conversation. However, slight defects of hearing do have significance in indicating a condition which if not remedied may eventually mean serious impairment or complete loss of hearing. The number of school children in Michigan who should be put into special classes for the deaf and hard of hearing has not yet been definitely determined. But the large number known to have defective hearing and the small number receiving special education in even the most progressive cities seems to indicate that no city has yet succeeded in providing special education for all school children seriously handicapped by defective hearing. Of the ten cities in Michigan which in 1921-1922 had special classes for the deaf and hard of hearing, Traverse City had the largest ratio of pupils enrolled in special classes to total population. This city with a population of about eleven thousand had an enrollment of sixteen pupils in classes for the deaf and hard of hearing.

If this ratio holds good for the state as a whole there are more than five thousand pupils who in justice to themselves and to others should receive their education wholly or in part in special classes. Yet in 1921-1922 there were enrolled in the special classes in public schools for the deaf and hard of hearing only 315 pupils, and in the Michigan School for the Deaf at Flint a little less than that number. That is, in special classes in the public schools and in our state school for the deaf combined we are caring for only about six hundred pupils, or probably about 12 per cent of the total number that should receive special education.

Under the law enacted in 1923 (Appendix A) state aid may be granted to every school district that has enough deaf and hard of hearing pupils to form a special class with an average attendance of not less than five pupils. The board of education of any school district that does not have enough children who are deaf or hard of hearing to form a special class may pay the tuition of these children to a school maintaining such a class. Every city of five thousand inhabitants doubtless has enough children to form a special class, and communities of much less population may be able to form special classes by receiving the deaf and hard of hearing from the smaller school districts. In the state of Michigan there are sixty cities with a population of five thousand inhabitants or more, comprising almost 58 per cent of the total population of the state, yet only ten of these cities are making special provision for the education of the deaf and hard of hearing. Since it is now possible to educate the deaf and hard of hearing in special classes with no greater cost to the local community than if they remained in the regular grades, there seems to be no valid excuse for failure to provide these children with the type of education best suited to their needs.

The simplest method of discovering the children who are defective in hearing is to have the teacher refer to the school physician for examination not merely all who are thought to be of defective hearing, but those as well who have discharging ears, or complain of earache or noises in the head. A strained look in the face, head turned so that one ear is nearer the speaker than the other, apparent attention to the lips of the speaker, unusual mistakes in dictation, and loudness or peculiar quality of voice, are all symptoms of defective hearing.

However, a better method is to have the teachers test the hearing of all the children in the elementary grades and refer to the school physician for examination all cases found by these tests to be of defective hearing. By this method many children of impaired hearing will be discovered who otherwise would escape detection. Experience in those states where teachers are required by law periodically to test the hearing and vision of school children has demonstrated that they are able to give these tests in a very satisfactory manner. However, in making a survey to find the children who are of defective hearing it should be borne in mind that the majority of deaf children found in the public schools were either born deaf or lost their hearing before the age of compulsory school attendance. This means that there are many deaf children five or six years of age who are not in school. A special effort should be made to get these children in school for if the speech of the deaf child is to be developed under the most favorable conditions, he should be in the special class at least by the time he is five or six years of age. Much also can be done for the deaf child of pre-school age through the instruction of his parents in regard to his care and training. The importance of early special training in speech development is indicated by the fact that fewer than half of the persons ten years of age or over who were born deaf or who lost their hearing in early childhood are able to use speech as a means of communication.

All cases of suspected impairment of hearing referred by the teachers to the school physician for examination and found by him to be of defective hearing, should be sent to an ear specialist for a more complete examination. A record of this examination should be in the hands of the special teacher in order that she may know the nature and extent of the defect and the character of the treatment required. For it is part of her work to see that the recommendations of the specialist are carried out.

It is also important that all pupils admitted to the special class for the deaf and hard of hearing have their vision tested. Vision in the deaf does in large measure the work of hearing. Hence, any defects of vision should, if possible, be corrected at once; otherwise the child is seriously handicapped in learning speech and lip-reading.

The average number of pupils per teacher enrolled in city day schools and classes for the deaf in the United States for the school year 1921-1922 was eight. Usually pupils placed in a special class for the deaf receive all their training and instruction from the teacher in charge of the special class. Where this plan is followed it is generally recognized that to secure the best results one teacher should not be expected to handle more than eight or ten pupils even though some of them are only hard of hearing. In some of the large cities the pupils are divided into two groups; the deaf and those seriously defective of hearing who are segregated into special classes or schools; and the hard of hearing who remain in the regular grades, but are given lessons in lip-reading by the special teacher. Of course where the special teacher is held responsible for lip-reading alone she can instruct a large number of pupils, the number depending on how well graded the pupils are, and the length and number of lessons given in lip reading per week. A satisfactory method of handling the situation in a school system where there are not enough deaf and hard of hearing children for more than one specia'

13

teacher, is to have all the hard of hearing pupils who stand in need of instruction in lip-reading transferred to the school in which the special class for the deaf is located. They would remain in the regular grade rooms and report to the special teacher merely for lessons in lip-reading.

It is desirable that the classroom for the deaf and hard of hearing be of about standard size, even though it is only occupied by a small number of pupils. The large room is better for speech work; it provides the necessary space for simple physical exercises and marching; and it makes it possible for the pupils to sit where the light is most favorable. The lighting of the classroom should be exceptionally good, for it is impossible to teach lip-reading and speech production satisfactorily in a poorly lighted room. What is said in regard to the location and lighting of the classroom for sight saving classes applies with equal force to the classroom for the deaf and hard of hearing. The classroom should be furnished with movable seats in order that space may be made available for physical exercise and rhythm work. The movable seats also make it possible for the pupil to change his position as may be necessary to secure the best light. An abundance of blackboard space should be provided as written work looms large in the education of the deaf and hard of hearing. Large, clearly defined wall charts are also to be considered as part of the essential equipment. A large wall mirror artificially lighted is necessary for the work in speech development. A piano of good quality is part of the indispensable equipment, since vibration plays such an important part in the development of speech and a sense of rhythm in those so deaf that they cannot be guided by the sound of the voice.

Since the aim in the education of the deaf is to prepare them to live happily and successfully with those of normal hearing, the course of study is essentially that of the regular grades with the emphasis placed on the development of speech and training in lip-reading along with special attention to health and physical development. The usual practice, as previously stated, is to have the special teacher take complete charge of the training and instruction of the deaf in all subjects at least during the early years of their school life. This is desirable as the congenitally deaf, and those who acquire deafness during the first three years of life, are usually retarded in their development one or more years by the time they have reached the age of six. Necessarily then the early years of the deaf child's school life are spent in acquiring knowledge the hearing child already possesses, and in developing speech which by this time is highly developed in the child of normal hearing. This means that the work of the special teacher is focussed during the early years of the deaf child's school life on teaching him lip-reading and in developing his speech. While in theory the aim is to develop speech and lip-reading to such an extent that the deaf child can successfully be returned to the regular grades, in practice this aim is realized in the

14

elementary schools only in a small percentage of cases. But the deaf child of average ability who continues his education beyond the elementary grades should be able to make normal progress in the regular high school or vocational school. However, while in the elementary grades, it is possible for the deaf child who is a good lip reader to work with children of normal hearing in those subjects where the emphasis is placed on doing rather than saying. Since it is so desirable for the deaf to have contacts with children of normal hearing where this can be done without undue embarrassment or discouragement, all classes and schools for the deaf should be located in or in connection with schools for the hearing.

The case is quite different when it comes to the training and instruction of those who are only hard of hearing. These pupils hear, but hear ordinary conversation imperfectly. Usually their speech is not greatly impaired. The chief work of the special teacher is to train them in lip-reading, but at the same time she is held responsible for the improvement of their speech. There is no good reason why these pupils should not remain in the regular grades and merely report to the special teacher for lessons in lip-reading and in speech improvement. In fact it is not desirable for them to sit in the special room where they are compelled to listen to the imperfect speech of the deaf, for one of the problems in the education of the hard of hearing is to prevent deterioration of speech, especially in those who have progressive defects of hearing.

The training and instruction of the congenitally deaf is doubtless the most difficult task that confronts any teacher. To succeed in this work requires a rare combination of personal qualities along with an unusual technical training. To labor long years to develop speech in the deaf requires and enthusiasm, optimism, and patience coupled with a love for the child that few possess. On the side of training it is necessary for the teacher to have a general and professional education as good as that possessed by the teacher of the regular grades and, in addition, she should have a technical knowledge of the anatomy and physiology of the organs of speech and hearing, a thorough knowledge of the causes of deafness, an acquaintance with the history of the education of the deaf, a working knowledge of the best methods of teaching the deaf, and above all a thorough knowledge of the deaf child. Furthermore it is important that the teacher of the deaf have had successful experience in teaching children of normal hearing if she is going to succeed in educating the deaf to lead a happy independent life with those of normal hearing. The teacher of the special class for the deaf and hard of hearing has a fine opportunity to do much in encouraging parents to send their handicapped children to the special class at the age of five or six instead of waiting until they have reached the age of compulsory school attendance. She also can be of great assistance to the parents of deaf children of pre-school age in suggesting to them the best methods of caring for and training these children until they become old enough to enter the special class. The teacher also can render a real service to the community by pointing out that scarlet fever, meningitis, brain fever, measles, and diphtheria are some of the preventable diseases that are causing a large percentage of deafness among children of pre-school age, and that catarrh and common colds, if neglected, lead to the impairment of hearing. If the teacher constantly bears in mind that no matter how effective the instruction and training of the deaf and hard of hearing may be, the handicap can never be wholly removed—that prevention is a thousand times more effective than any attempted cure—her influence will extend far beyond the classroom.

What shall be done for the education of the deaf and hard of hearing in those school districts which do not have enough such pupils to form a special class? It is hardly likely that many towns and cities of less than five thousand inhabitants have enough deaf and hard of hearing children to warrant a special class. Yet in the rural districts and towns of less than five thousand inhabitants, which include more than 40 per cent of the population of the state, there are probably not less than two thousand deaf and hard of hearing children who stand in need of special education.

One answer to the question raised is to send them to the state school for the deaf at Flint, but, unfortunately, the state school is now almost filled to capacity. Even if there were room in the state school for all of these children, many would not enter because most parents are unwilling to send a child who is merely hard of hearing to a school for the deaf, for they do not like the idea of having him identified with the deaf. Even the parents of deaf children who recognize the importance of early education in the development of speech are reluctant to send away from home to school children only five or six years of age whose handicap makes them appear even younger.

A partial solution would be to have one district form a special class with the understanding that all the deaf from adjacent districts were to be sent to that class. This method would insure a class large enough to secure state aid. The disadvantage would be that many children would have long distances to travel or would have to live during the week in the district where the special class was located. However, this would be much better in most cases than to send the child to the state school where he would have no opportunity to visit his home for months at a time.

In the case of the hard of hearing another method might be used that would obviate the necessity of children travelling long distances; that is, to have in each school district one center where the hard of hearing pupils would go for their lessons in lip-reading which would be given by a special teacher who would serve several districts. This is the gen-

16

eral plan pursued in some of the large cities. The centers are established in a number of schools and the hard of hearing pupils from adjacent schools come to these centers at certain times for their lessons in lip-reading. This plan makes it possible for one teacher to instruct all the hard of hearing pupils who are scattered over a large territory. Were each child to receive only two lessons per week in lip-reading, as is the case in some cities, a large number of pupils could be taught by the one teacher. However, it would be necessary for her to devote some time at least to speech improvement in the hard of hearing.

Even if the suggestions made were to be fully carried out, there would still be a very important work for our state school. There will always be some deaf and hard of hearing in the small districts and in isolated communities who cannot be educated satisfactorily in the public schools. The state school is also the place for the dependent and neglected deaf, for those who come from undesirable homes, and for those who because of certain traits of character stand in need of the restraint and close supervision possible in a state school. There are also the deaf who need certain kinds of vocational training which are not found in the home community; these would profit from the vocational training offered in our state school. Finally there are children who apparently are unable to learn speech; these might be given advantageously the opportunity of learning language by the manual method in our state school for the deaf. After a fair trial those found to be incapable of making appreciable progress should be returned to their homes or sent to the institution for the feebleminded. Many fail to realize that there is no necessary relation between deafness and feeblemindedness. The institution for the feebleminded is the place for mentally deficient children, whether they are deaf or of normal hearing. Close cooperation between the state school for the deaf and the public school classes for the deaf and hard of hearing means a better education for these handicapped children.

Special training for the deaf has long been accepted as necessary and the results have abundantly justified the great expenditure of money, time, and effort. However, the people are not quite so clear as to the significance of special education for the hard of hearing. The tendency has been to accept impairment of hearing as a misfortune for which there is no help, but with the formation of classes in lip-reading for deaf adults as well as for hard of hearing children the people are beginning to realize that impairment of hearing may in large measure be overcome through careful training in lip-reading. The results thus obtained have been most reassuring. By means of lip-reading children failing in their work have become successful; others hopelessly discouraged have taken a new lease on life. The following quotations from pupils in lip-reading classes of the public schools are significant: "Now, I understand everything my teacher says"; "I got my spelling lesson today when she gave it out and this was the first time I ever got it"; "I got better marks this month"; "Lip-reading has helped me lots". These quotations indicate what training in lip-reading means to the children of impaired hearing.

SELECTED REFERENCES

Best, Harry, *The Deaf.* Thomas V. Crowell Company, New York, 1914

Farrar, A., *Arnold on the Education of the Deaf.* A manual for Teachers. Second Edition. It may be secured from the Volta Bureau, Washington, D. C.

Gulick, L. H. and Ayres, L. P., *Medical Inspection of Schools.* Charities Publication Committee, New York, 1913. Contains instructions to teachers for giving tests of hearing

Horn, John Louis, *The Education of Exceptional Children.* The Century Company, New York, 1924

Wright, John D., *What the Mother of a Deaf Child Ought to Know.* Frederick A. Stokes Company, New York, 1915

Deaf-Mutes in the United States, 1920. Government Printing Office, Washington, D. C., 1923

Wallin, J. E. W., *Education of Handicapped Children.* Houghton Mifflin Company, Chicago, 1924

III. THE CRIPPLED

In 1916 under the auspices of the Welfare Federation of Cleveland was conducted the first city wide survey of cripples in the United States. As a result of this house to house canvass it was found that Cleveland with a total population of about 674,000 had 4,186 cripples, approximately six per thousand, and that 25 per cent of the cripples were between 5 and 20 years of age. In other words, on the average there were 1.5 crippled children of school age per thousand of general population. The surveys that have been made in Michigan during the past two years under the auspices of the Michigan Society for Crippled Children seem to indicate that in this state there are about two crippled children between 6 and 20 years of age per thousand of general population. That the number of crippled children in Michigan appears to be greater than in Cleveland is probably due in large part to the difference in the definition of the term. In the Cleveland survey a cripple was defined as an individual handicapped through lack of normal use of skeleton or skeletal muscles, while in Michigan the definition has been broadened to include serious cardiopathic cases as well.

Just what percentage of those who are crippled stand in need of special education has not yet been definitely determined. However, it is probable that about half of these children would profit greatly from special education, although at present few if any cities have that large a percentage of crippled children enrolled in special classes. Still we have little reason to think that any large city as yet is adequately providing for the education of all its crippled children. It is only through the kind of work that is being carried on by the Michigan Society for Crippled Children so generously sponsored by the Rotary Clubs, that the exact number of crippled children in need of special education will be brought to light.

If there is one crippled child per thousand of general population who stands in need of special education, it is evident that every city in Michigan of 10,000 inhabitants or above has enough crippled children to form at least one special class. For under the law enacted in 1923 (Appendix B) it is possible to secure state aid for the education of crippled children in special classes who are between 6 and 20 years of age as long as there is an actual attendance of not less than five such children. The need for the development of this type of education is apparent from the fact that only five of the twenty-eight cities in Michigan with a population of 10,000 or above are providing special education for these handicapped children. The total enrollment of crippled children in the special classes of these five cities is less than five hundred although there are doubtless more than three thousand crippled children in the state who could be greatly helped through special education.

Infantile paralysis and tuberculosis of the bones are the two great scourges of childhood, since more children are crippled by these two diseases than by all other causes combined. Statistics from the special schools for cripples of Chicago and Detroit, and from the Cleveland and Michigan surveys show that infantile paralysis alone accounts for at least 40 per cent of all the crippled children, that tuberculosis of the bones comes next claiming from 5 to 20 per cent, and that spastic paralysis, a disease which so frequently cripples the mind as well as the body, accounts for from 8 to 15 per cent. In other words, approximately two-thirds of all the crippled children have been disabled by these three diseases. In the Cleveland survey it was found that only 16 per cent of the crippled children were born crippled. This means that over 80 per cent of all the crippled children have been disabled through disease or accident, both in large measure preventable. Evidently the task of special education is a twofold one, cure and prevention.

A. The Crippled in Large Cities

In most of the large cities that have made special provision for the care, treatment, and education of crippled children the work has been centralized in special schools. The five special schools for cripples in

Chicago, the Nellie Leland School in Detroit, and the recently completed Stocking School for Crippled Children in Grand Rapids are cases in point. The possible advantages of such centralization are: buildings constructed to meet the needs of the crippled child, better facilities for medical examinations and for curative and corrective treatment, the departmentalization of instruction, better classification for the purposes of instruction, and facilities for pre-vocational training. In some cities the transportation problem is simplified by having all the cripples in one center.

On the other hand, New York City has placed more emphasis on the development of the special class or classes in connection with the regular elementary schools than on the centralization of the education of cripples into special buildings constructed for that purpose. The special class makes it possible for the crippled child to identify himself with the regular elementary school and participate in its activities to the extent of his capacity.

But whether crippled children are cared for in special classes or in special schools, in the most progressive school systems special education has come to mean not only transportation to and from school, but responsibility for medical examinations, corrective treatment, proper feeding, braces and artificial limbs, and suitable vocational training, as well as home instruction for helpless cripples. All of these things may not be done by the school but all are being attempted under the direction of the school. In one year in New York City the department in charge of the education of cripples enlisted the cooperation of the surgeons and social service nurses of thirty-three hospitals and clinics and of forty-five other associations in treating and caring for crippled children.

All candidates either before or at the time of admission to the school for cripples should be given a general medical examination in order, first, to determine whether any are suffering from infections or contagious diseases, and second, to find those who stand in need of orthopedic treatment. However, this examination should not be confined to candidates for admission to the special school, but should include all cripples in the elementary schools, for it has been found that many of these children who are not candidates for the special school stand in need of corrective treatment. In fact, it is surprising how many parents in our large cities are not even aware of what could be done by surgery and corrective treatment for their crippled children. The medical examination of all crippled children makes it possible to select for the special school those who stand most in need of transportation, corrective treatment, or pre-vocational training.

Buildings used for the care and education of crippled children range from the ordinary elementary school building to those specially constructed for this work. The characteristic features of the latter are wide hallways and exits, inclined ways and large elevators, if the building is more than one story in height; classrooms, gymnasium, baths and toilet facilities on the same floor; an open-air room equipped with cots and blankets, a lunch room, an assembly room, an industrial room, and a room for medical examinations and corrective treatment equipped for physiotherapy work. The classrooms are usually equipped with movable adjustable seats. In addition wheel chairs are provided for the more helpless children, who are not able to walk with the aid of crutches.

The crippled children not able to use the street cars are usually transported by means of police patrols or automobile busses. In some cases the busses are owned and operated by the board of education; again the contract for the transportation of crippled children is let to private parties. The almost universal practice is to have two persons on each bus, a driver and an attendant. Sometimes the latter is a police officer; again a woman acts in this capacity. Probably the most satisfactory practice is where the board of education owns and operates the busses as they can then be used not only to convey children to and from school but also to take them to museums, theaters, parks, and to hospitals for treatment.

The work of a school for crippled children may be considered under three headings, corrective, academic, and vocational. The corrective work which is under the general supervision of the orthopedic surgeon embraces all that is done directly to overcome the physical defect. It includes both operative and other corrective treatment for the child not under the care of a private physician. The chief function of the school in connection with operative treatment is to persuade the parents to have the needed operation performed and this in many cases is by no means an easy task. The corrective treatment in the well equipped school consists of definite forms of physiotherapy—such as muscle training for infantile paralysis, coordinating exercises for spastic paralysis cases, corrective exercises for children with scoliosis, and massage and special exercises for various other orthopedic conditions. This is all done by physiotherapy aides working under the direction of the orthopedic surgeon. The special class teachers consult with the physiotherapist, so that none of the various classroom and occupational activities may be harmful to the child, but that they may, just as far as possible, serve as corrective exercise. Much attention is given to improving the general health of the children by means of lunches, rest, and fresh air. This is especially necessary in cases of the tuberculous children.

The academic work in schools for cripples differs little from that of the regular elementary school except that more attention is given to health instruction. It is quite necessary that the regular course of study be followed as many children after corrective treatment are returned to the

21

regular grades. In a large well graded school for cripples it is possible for the academic teacher successfully to instruct as many as twenty-five pupils. It is important that the academic work be taught by teachers capable of stimulating the brighter boys and girls to continue their education so as to fit themselves for vocations where their physical disability in large measure ceases to be a handicap.

The educational retardation among cripples is much greater than among other children of like age. While this is due to a great extent to late entrance and irregular attendance, mental retardation is also a factor. In the Cleveland survey it was found that 8 per cent of the crippled children were feebleminded. In schools for cripples with a large percentage of spastic paralysis cases, mental retardation is a serious problem.

In the case of cripples whose disabilities can be corrected there is no special vocational problem. The same is true of the boys and girls who are permanently crippled but of unusual ability, but the case is quite different with cripples of average or less than average ability who necessarily will be compelled to engage in occupations where more or less manual activity is required. However, if a variety of vocational training is offered, most of these children can be prepared for occupations in which their particular disabilities will handicap them the least. Chicago offers training for cripples in woodworking, toy-making, printing, weaving of textiles, cobbling, brace making, clay modeling, millinery, sewing, and cooking. As yet little has been accomplished in training subnormal cripples to become even in part self-supporting.

B. The Crippled in Small Communities

The problem of special education of crippled children in the small community is quite different from that of the large city. The small number of such children precludes the possibility of careful grading. In the same class will be found children differing widely in age and achievement. In addition children crippled by infantile paralysis, tuberculosis of the bones, spastic paralysis as well as cardiopathic cases are all apt to be found in the one special class, although these different types need different treatment in both academic and corrective work. Again it is not possible to have a full time physiotherapy aide for corrective treatment when there is only one special class of crippled children; and in the small community part-time assistance of this kind is usually not to be had. Then, too, the necessary facilities for surgical treatment of orthopedic cases are usually lacking, and if the child is sent to a large city hospital for the necessary operation, the follow-up treatment is apt to be neglected upon return to the home community. Neither is it possible in the small community to offer training in a variety of occupations.

This does not mean that special education of crippled children in smaller communities is impracticable, but rather that the plan of conducting this work must necessarily differ from that of the large city. Special education even in a community that does* not have enough crippled children for more than one class could well attempt the following:

1. To locate all crippled children of school and pre-school age. Careful surveys have resulted in the discovering of crippled children not generally known to exist.

2. To acquaint parents with the possibilities of corrective treatment for their crippled children, and to persuade them to have necessary operations performed.

3. To furnish home instruction to bed-ridden cripples of school age.

4. To provide for the transportation of crippled children to and from school.

5. To provide an attractive, well-located classroom properly equipped for the instruction, training, and corrective treatment of crippled children.

6. To provide the necessary occupational training for crippled children by working with the supervisor of vocational rehabilitation at Lansing.

7. To enlist the cooperation of the various civic and welfare organizations and direct their efforts into those channels that will be of most value to the crippled child. The work of such agencies is apt to be sporadic and accomplish little unless directed by one who has a thorough grasp of the problem.

8. To make use of the Michigan Society for Crippled Children at Ann Arbor. This society is always glad to assist the local community in every way possible.

9. To secure from the hospitals to which local cases have been sent for operations, information relative to the needed after-treatment.

10. To arouse the local community to the importance of fighting infantile paralysis and tuberculosis, which are blighting the lives of so many children.

The first steps necessary to carry out the above suggestions are the discovery and examination of all crippled children in the community. In many places these steps have already been taken under the direction of the Michigan Society for Crippled Children assisted by civic and welfare organizations. The next step is the formation of the special class for crippled children of school age who need corrective treatment, conveyance to and from school, or any other special service.

The special class should be in a regular elementary school in order that the crippled children may have the opportunity of participating as far as possible in the activities of children not handicapped. The classroom should be on the first floor near the entrance to obviate the necessity of climbing stairs and to minimize the danger from fire. It should be attractive, well lighted and ventilated, and equipped with movable adjustable seats. It is desirable to have a railing around the classroom to make it easier for the children to move about and work at the blackboard. A few wheel chairs should be provided for the more helpless children and cots and blankets for all who need a rest period.

The room for medical examinations and corrective work should be adjacent to the classroom. It should have hot and cold water, and be equipped with scales, electric baker, and massage table. Additional equipment can be added as needed. However, much of the corrective treatment can be done in the gymnasium and in connection with manual work. The equipment and supplies needed will be determined by the type of case found in the special class, and also by the availability of hospitals. In New York City much of the corrective work is done in hospitals that in other cities is attempted in connection with the special school for cripples.

The course of study followed in the special class is usually that of the regular grades with more emphasis on hygiene and physical education. In some places all the academic instruction is given by the special class teacher; in other places the children recite to some extent with the regular grades, and, as far as possible, participate in the general activities of the school. The latter plan of conducting the special class not only has a good effect on the crippled child in making him feel that he is not so different from other children, but on the other children as well in showing them what a child can do even though handicapped. It also makes them more considerate in their treatment of the crippled child, thereby making it easier for him to rise above his handicap. But these results can be obtained only under favorable conditions. To have crippled children, handicapped in mind as well as in body, attempt to associate on equal terms with other children simply increases the gulf that separates the two groups. The best results can be obtained only where the brighter cripples are brought into competition in school work with other children, for the other children then discover that the crippled child whom they thought to be inferior to themselves in all things is equal if not superior to them in many things.

The corrective work attempted in the special class of a small school system will naturally depend on the type of case found, and the facilities for corrective treatment available in the community outside of the school. If a physiotherapist cannot be secured the regular teacher of physical education and the school nurse should be able under the direction of the orthopedic surgeon appointed by the board of education to carry out all corrective work that it is advisable to undertake in the school.

Children needing operations and unusual treatment whose parents are unable to pay can be sent to the University hospital at Ann Arbor where they will be treated and cared for at state expense. (Appendix C). The special class teacher should send the school record of any such child to the superintendent of the University hospital on or before admission in order that his school work may be continued during the period he spends in the hospital, and she should request that at the time of his discharge she be given full information in regard to his school progress while in the hospital and the kind of after-treatment needed. She should consider it an important part of her work to see that the after treatment recommended is carried out. The surveys of the Michigan Society for Crippled Children have brought to light many cases that have received comparatively little benefit from operations performed because of the neglect of after treatment.

The permanently crippled child of average or less than average intelligence presents a real vocational problem. In respect to the most serious cases the state department of vocational rehabilitation should be consulted. However, the attempt should be made to prepare most of these children to earn a living in the home community. They are much more apt to secure and hold a job in the home town where they are widely known than in a strange city where competition is keen. There are in every community many simple occupations that require little physical activity and no great amount of mental ability. Newspaper stands, boot blacking establishments, and fruit stands can frequently be managed just as successfully by the crippled as by those not handicapped in body. Why not in the local community give the preference to the physically handicapped when it comes to the limited number of trades and occupations in which they can succeed? Through the civic organizations a strong sentiment in this direction could be developed. Other things being equal we trade with our friends in preference to strangers. Why not count the crippled our friends? But it is important that other things be equal. It must not be a case of paying ten cents for a one cent pencil because it is sold by a cripple. He must give value received; for we soon cease to buy from our friends if they charge us more than we would have to pay elsewhere. Even under favorable, conditions, to be successful the cripple must in a measure rise above his handicap. If he is sour and pessimistic, failure is inevitable; if he smiles, success is assured. In the last analysis his handicap is more mental than physical. The development of right attitudes is the most important and the most difficult problem in the pre-vocational training of crippled children.

Home instruction should be provided for helpless cripples of school age. The usual practice is for the home teacher to give each child two or more lessons per week, each an hour and a half in length. The home teacher is also expected to use her influence to secure for the child proper care and treatment. In New York City most of the home instruction is given by full-time teachers appointed for that purpose, but in the outlying schools this work is done after school hours and on Saturdays by the regular elementary teachers who receive extra compensation. In the small community work of this kind could be done either by the special teacher or under her direction. Experience has shown that there is no child that appreciates instruction more than the helpless cripple confined to his home.

The success of the work for crippled children in any small community will depend in large measure on the teacher of the special class, for she should be the leader in that community in all that pertains to cripple-prevention, correction, education, and placement. The person selected for this work should have had previous successful teaching experience in the regular grades and special training and instruction for the teaching and treatment of crippled children. The latter should include a knowledge of the causes and prevention of the diseases that cripple children, training in handwork and corrective gymnastics, and some knowledge of the vocations suitable for cripples. In addition to the necessary training the special teacher must have certain personal qualities if she is to have much influence outside of the classroom. A pleasing personality and ability for leadership will do much in helping her to secure the cooperation of the home and the support of the civic and welfare organizations in her work for the crippled child.

SELECTED REFERENCES

Abt, H. E., *The Care, Cure and Education of the Crippled Child.* International Society for Crippled Children, Elyria, Ohio, 1924

The Crippled Child, A bi-monthly magazine published by the International Society for Crippled Children, Elyria, Ohio

Hare, Helen, *A Study of Handicapped Children.* Indiana University Studies No. 41, June 1919

Horn, John Louis, *The Education of Exceptional Children.* The Century Company, New York, 1924

Solenberg, Edith Reeves, *Public School Classes for Crippled Children.* Bureau of Education, Bulletin, 1918. No. 10

Wallin, J. E. W., *The Education of Handicapped Children.* Houghton Mifflin Company, Chicago, 1924

Wright, Lucy and Hamburger, Amy M., *Education and Occupations of Cripples, Juvenile and Adult* (A Survey of All the Cripples of Cleveland, Ohio, in 1916.) The Red Cross Institute for Crippled and Disabled Men, 311 Fourth Avenue, New York City

IV. THE DEFECTIVE IN SPEECH

A pleasant, well modulated voice and the ability to express easily and effectively in spoken language one's ideas and feelings are among the most striking characteristics of a cultured and educated person. Yet in our country as compared with Europe these characteristics are altogether too rare even among those who have enjoyed the advantages of so-called higher education. These things are in large measure determined by the early training of the individual in the home and in the school. It seems strange that during the early years of a child's school life when the organs of speech are plastic, when defects can more easily be corrected than at any later time, so little emphasis has been placed on the development of speech and so much on reading and writing. For after all the average adult speaks one hundred words for every one he reads or writes. His success and happiness in life are conditioned only in small measure by his ability to read and write well but in marked degree by his ability to express his thoughts and feelings in a pleasing and effective manner. If well developed speech means so much, how great is the handicap of defective speech which compels the person of superior intellectual ability and of fine personal qualities all too often to accept an inferior station in life, to suffer constant disappointment and humiliation!

One teacher when asked why he did not devote more attention to the development of better speech in the members of his class who were noticeably deficient in that respect replied that he found it much easier to improve their written work than to correct their speech. And in that he was quite right, for these boys fourteen to sixteen years of age had passed the period when their speech could most easily have been corrected. With so much emphasis placed on reading and writing it is small wonder that little has been done in so many school systems to correct defects of speech. Yet the school cooperating with the home has the power to improve the speech of a nation.

The need for such cooperation is revealed by the fact that no less than 75 per cent of the school children with speech defects had them at the time they first entered school. But many parents have said: "Why bother with these defects as time will correct them?" It is true that many of the minor defects gradually disappear as the child grows older. Just as it is true that most children recover from the mumps and measles without the aid of a physician, yet the wise parent calls in the physician, for all children do not recover and many others are handicapped for life. Why allow a child to suffer from a defect of speech any longer than is necessary? For in a large percentage of cases the defect is not corrected without expert assistance, and the longer the assistance is withheld, the slower and more difficult the correction. The percentage of the more serious defects of speech even tends to increase from the lower to the

27

higher grades of the elementary school. Wallin found in his survey of the public schools of St. Louis that the percentage of stutterers in the seventh and eighth grades was one and one-half times as great as in the first and second grades.

It is generally conceded that at least 2 per cent of school children have speech defects so serious that they need special instruction. From one-third to one-half of these cases are stutterers. In fact more than 3 per cent of the pupils enrolled in the public schools of Grand Rapids are receiving special instruction in speech correction. In Detroit the percentage is 1.8 with a waiting list that would increase it to about that of Grand Rapids. Possibly the large percentage of children of foreign parentage in these two cities makes the percentage of speech correction cases higher than would be found in most of the other towns and cities of Michigan. However, it is probable that at least 2 per cent of the school population in our rural districts and in our small towns and cities have defects of speech sufficiently serious to require special instruction.

The preliminary selection of pupils for speech improvement classes is usually made by the teachers of the regular grades with the assistance of the principal. Those selected are then examined by the speech improvement teachers to see if they really stand in need of special instruction. The cases of minor speech defects that the grade teacher can correct are not taken into the speech improvement classes, but the grade teacher is given instruction as to how to handle these cases. However, the practice in regard to the type of pupil put into the speech improvement class varies in different cities. In Rochester, New York, since they do not have enough special teachers to care for all children who have defective speech, they select most of their cases from the upper grades, as the supervisor of speech improvement classes believes that many of the younger children will succeed in overcoming their defects without special assistance. In Boston the speech improvement classes are composed almost exclusively of stutterers. Since they are unable to care for all, they deem it wise to take the cases suffering from the most serious defects; hence they select the stutterers. In New York City since they do not have teachers enough to provide for all children with defective speech, they do not attempt to cover the entire city each year, but do endeavor to make adequate provision for all serious cases in the schools they reach. On the other hand, in Detroit and Grand Rapids the attempt is made to reach all cases of defective speech that stand in need of special instruction. In this Grand Rapids has been more successful than Detroit, although Detroit is caring for a larger percentage of such cases than most of the large cities. In these two cities special attention is given to the younger children, for it is always easier to correct an incipient defect of speech than one which has become confirmed. This is especially true of stutterers. If we give special instruction to the children in the first and second grades who have defects of speech, in a few years there will not be many in the upper grades that will stand in need of speech correction.

While it is not necessary that all children placed in speech improvement classes be given a medical examination, yet it is of the highest importance that the teachers of such classes refer to the physician all cases that have organic defects of any kind. Poor health, diseased tonsils, adenoids, and decayed teeth are all factors that tend to make more difficult the correction of defective speech. If the teacher has had the right kind of training and experience she will have little difficulty in picking out most of the cases that should be referred to the physician for medical treatment.

The greatest difficulty is not in finding the cases that stand in need of medical treatment, but in convincing the parents of the necessity for such treatment. The teacher should regard this as a very important part of her work.

In the large cities certain schools well located are designated as speech centers and the pupils who stand in need of speech correction are sent to these centers from the adjacent schools. In Boston there is only one center for each speech improvement teacher, but in most cities each teacher has two or more centers. Other things being equal, the more centers per teacher the less distance the pupils will have to go and the easier it will be to get the younger children into the speech correction classes. Another great advantage of having the teacher give instruction in a number of different schools is that it brings her in closer contact with the regular grade teachers. However, if the number of pupils in any one center is very small the grading for group instruction becomes difficult.

Any well lighted classroom may be used for speech correction work but a room of standard size is preferable if it is to be used exclusively for this work as it allows the necessary space for group exercises. The room should be equipped with movable seats, a piano, a large mirror, blackboards, and a bookcase for the regular grade books and books on speech correction.

The speech improvement teacher devotes all of her time to speech correction work and is not held responsible for the progress of her pupils in the regular grade subjects. This means that all speech correction cases sit in the regular grades and go to the special teacher merely for assistance in overcoming their speech defects. This is more satisfactory than segregating speech correction pupils into special classes for training and instruction in all subjects by the speech improvement teacher, as it enables her to handle a much larger number of cases and at the same time keeps the child of defective speech in a normal environment while overcoming his handicap.

As speech correction work is conducted in most of the large cities one teacher is able to instruct at least one hundred children per week. Among the important factors that determine the number of pupils one teacher can instruct are the frequency of the lessons, the length of the lessons, and the number of pupils taught in a group. There is great diversity of practice in regard to all three factors. The number of lessons ranges from one to five per week, the length of the lesson from twenty minutes to a half day, and the number of pupils taught at one time from one to fifteen. However, in most cities the speech correction cases receive two lessons per week from forty-five minutes to an hour and a half in length in groups of eight to twelve pupils.

It is not best to require the teacher of speech correction work to devote all her time to class or individual instruction. Better results can be secured by having her spend some time in the grade rooms from which her pupils come, observing how they react under actual classroom conditions and in instructing the grade teacher how to correct minor defects of speech. In one large city the speech improvement teachers teach no pupils on one day of each week. This day is spent in the regular grade rooms, in examining candidates for speech improvement classes, and in visiting the homes to enlist the cooperation of the parents. Since in most cities the child does not receive more than two lessons per week from the speech improvement teacher, much depends on his carrying out the instructions and faithfully practicing the exercises the teacher has given him. To get the desired results it is necessary for the teacher to visit the home of the child and encourage the parents to do their part in assisting their child to correct his speech.

The results secured by speech improvement teachers have been very satisfactory in spite of the diversity of practice. Some cities have succeeded in correcting the defects of speech in more than three-fourths of the children placed in speech improvement classes. The time required depends upon the character of the defect, the age, ability and perseverance of the child, the cooperation of the home and the grade teacher, and on the skill of the special teacher. A good many defects are not corrected, generally not because the defect in itself is so serious, but rather because of the indifference of the home or the lack of effort on the part of the child. It must be frankly recognized that the correction and improvement of speech is a cooperative undertaking involving the child, the home, the regular school, and the special teacher.

Only teachers who have had successful experience in the elementary grades should be encouraged to prepare for speech improvement work by securing the necessary training and instruction. No teacher should enter this field who does not get along well with people, since to be successful she must work in close cooperation with the home, the physician, and the grade teacher. The speech improvement teacher generally receives fifty to two hundred dollars more salary per year than the regular grade teacher.

How shall the speech correction work be handled in the smaller school districts where there are not enough cases to require the full time of a speech improvement teacher? Generally it has been left to the regular grade teacher's who have been given no special training or instruction with the result that many children have left school handicapped for life with defects of speech that could have been corrected if they had been placed under the instruction of a properly trained speech improvement teacher.

There are different ways of solving this problem in the smaller school districts, but there is one element common to all solutions, and that is, the school or school district must have one teacher who has had special training for speech correction work. Where there is a class for the deaf it may be feasible in some instances to have the teacher of this class also take the speech correction work. In some places the teachers of lip-reading give instruction to those having defects of speech. Again it may be desirable to have the children with defective speech sent to the teacher of the special class for mentally retarded children for correction. In some places the coaching teacher has rendered excellent service in correcting defects of speech. Another plan is to have a successful first grade teacher who has had special training devote part of her time to speech correction work. No matter what plan is followed if we are going to equalize educational opportunity, it is imperative that every school system have at least one teacher who has had training for speech improvement work. She can instruct the other teachers in the correcting of the minor defects of speech so that only the more serious cases would fall to her lot. It is hard to overestimate the influence of one well trained enthusiastic teacher in arousing greater interest in better speech.

SELECTED REFERENCES

Blanton, S. D. and Blanton, M. G., *Speech Training for Children: The Hygiene of Speech.* The Century Company, New York, 1919

Scripture, E. W., *Stuttering, Lisping and Correction of the Speech of the Deaf* (Second Edition). Macmillan Company, New York, 1923

Swift, W. B., *Speech Defects in School Children and How to Treat Them.* Houghton Mifflin Company, Boston, 1918

Terman, Lewis M., *The Hygiene of the School Child.* Houghton Mifflin Company, Boston, 1914

Chicago Course of Study in Speech Correction. Board of Education, Chicago, Illinois

Detroit Course of Study in Speech Correction. Board of Education, Detroit, Michigan

V. THE MENTALLY RETARDED

In large cities special classes for children who are seriously retarded mentally are now regarded as a wise investment, for these classes not only relieve the regular grades of those who are interfering with the progress of others without making progress themselves, but at the same time they provide, for these retarded children, training and instruction suited to their capacity.

In some large cities there are two types of classes for the mentally retarded, one for the backward and the other for the subnormal. In classes for the subnormal are usually placed children with an intelligence quotient of less than seventy-five. This means that all pupils in these classes are seriously retarded mentally and that many of them are feebleminded. In the classes for the backward are found children of a higher level of intelligence, the intelligence quotient generally ranging from seventy-five to eighty-five or ninety, with some behavior and special disability cases of even greater intelligence.

A. The Subnormal

It is generally conceded that about 2 per cent of the children in the elementary schools are of such inferior intelligence that in justice to themselves and to others they should be educated in special schools or classes. In 1922-1923 the number of such children in special classes for subnormal pupils in the public schools of Grand Rapids was equal to 2.4 per cent of the total enrollment in the first eight grades. The corresponding figures for Detroit for the same year were 1.8 per cent with enough subnormal pupils on the waiting list to increase the total to more than 2 per cent. It may be said that in the smaller cities and in the rural districts the percentage of subnormal pupils is much smaller than in cities like Detroit and Grand Rapids. However, the results of the survey of rural schools made by a committee of the Michigan State Teachers' Association of which Professor C. M. Elliott* was chairman showed that the percentage of subnormal children in the rural districts is apparently as great as in the large cities. According to the judgment of the teachers 2 per cent of the children were incapable of learning school lessons because of lack of mental capacity, and in those schools where individual psychological examinations were given to all the pupils, 8 per cent were found to have an intelligence quotient of less than seventy-five.

The simplest if not the most satisfactory method of finding the pupils who should be in the special class for subnormals is to ask each teacher to pick out the subnormal pupils in her room. Unfortunately in many

*Elliott, C. M., *Backward and Deficient Children.* Department of Public Instruction, Lansing, 1918

cases instead of picking out those who are most seriously retarded mentally she picks out the ones that are giving her the most trouble, and the two are not always synonymous, for many of the trouble makers are not subnormal and many of the subnormal are not trouble makers. Again she frequently fails to take chronological age into consideration with the result that some pupils two or three years over-age are not even considered for the special class.

A better method is to make use of the age-grade distribution as well as the judgment of the teacher. All pupils two years or more over-age, those pupils in the first grade not doing satisfactory work whether over-age or not, and such others as the teacher may select, should be given a group intelligence test and those failing to make a satisfactory showing should then be given an individual psychological examination and all found to have an intelligence quotient below seventy-five, should be considered candidates for the special class. If there is not room in the special class for all the subnormal pupils the younger children should have the preference. The cause of special education has suffered much from the erroneous idea that a child must be retarded educationally three years or more before he should be put into a special class. Just as soon as it has been ascertained that a child does not have the capacity to do the regular grade work he should be drafted off into the special class. To wait until initiative and interest have been destroyed by repeated failure makes it impossible for the special class teacher to get satisfactory results.

All pupils admitted to the special class should have a medical examination. It is folly of the worst sort for a special teacher to spend her time attempting to train and instruct a child suffering from physical defects that could be corrected. Defective eyesight or hearing, diseased tonsils, adenoids, and malnutrition are some of the factors that make it difficult for the teacher to get results. Every special teacher should regard it as a very important aspect of her work to see that all defects are corrected as far as possible and that the child is kept in good physical condition. The special class teacher should have for every pupil in her class a record card showing the facts relative to previous history in school, and the results of the physical and mental examinations. The record of the pupil from term to term should be kept on this card.

The number of subnormal pupils that one teacher can satisfactorily train and instruct depends upon the extent to which the pupils differ in age, capacity, and attainment. It is evident, other things being equal, that if they range in age from seven to sixteen the problem is more difficult than where they are approximately of the same age, for even the interests of adolescents and pre-adolescents of the same mental age are not the same. Again they may be of nearly the same chronological age but differ widely in mental age which necessitates a difference in methods and subject-matter of instruction. Even when the subnormal pupils are much alike in respect to age and capacity they may differ widely in their attainments in that they have had different kinds of training in the home and in the school before entering the special class. Generally speaking, where the teacher has subnormal pupils differing widely in age and ability, she should not be expected to have more than fifteen to twenty in her class. Where they are segregated into special schools and classified according to age and ability, an average of twenty-five pupils to the teacher is probably not too great. The laws of New York State and New Jersey name fifteen as the maximum number of subnormal pupils to be taught by one teacher, and yet the practice in both states seems to be to increase the maximum beyond fifteen.

In large cities the tendency in the education of subnormal pupils is to keep the younger boys and girls together in special classes located in the regular grade schools, but to segregate the older boys and girls into separate special schools. The special school makes possible better classification, the departmentalization of instruction, and a greater variety of training. Most of the pupils in these schools come from the special classes in connection with the regular grade schools. Their failure in the special class to make sufficient progress to warrant their return to the regular grades removes in large measure the objections of the parents to their entering the special school. On the other hand, the advantages of having the special class for the younger pupils in the regular grade school are that parents do not object so seriously to special education, the pupils do not have so far to travel, and they can more easily be returned to the regular grades on trial. For after all, the special class in the elementary school should be regarded as a place where a child can be carefully studied before final disposition of the case is made.

The classroom for the younger subnormal children should be of standard size in order to provide the necessary space for physical training and manual activities and for equipment and supplies. Since the room is used for a variety of purposes it is desirable that it be furnished with movable seats. In addition to the standard supplies of an elementary grade room the special room should be provided with kindergarten supplies, one-half dozen Todd looms, 8x12 inches, a manual training bench with equipment, and with a greater variety of easy readers and supplementary textbooks than is usually found in an elementary grade room.

Where there are separate special schools for the older boys and girls it is desirable that each be provided with gymnasium, baths, lunchroom as well as with necessary classrooms, and that the school for boys be equipped for manual training, household mechanics, simple drawing, auto-mechanics, cobbling and plumbing, and that the school for girls be

34

equipped for cooking, sewing, laundering, dressmaking, and cafeteria work.

The young child who is committed to the special class for subnormal children should be regarded by the teacher as "x", the unknown quantity, the value of which is to be determined. It is unfair to the child for her to assume that because he was unable to keep up with pupils of his own age and has a low intelligence quotient that he never will be able to make good in the regular grades. For her, achievement under the most favorable conditions that she can create, must be taken as the ultimate criterion of the child's capacity. That this attitude on the part of the teacher is the only way of insuring equality of opportunity for the child committed to her charge, is shown by the fact that in the large cities where children are given both a medical and psychological examination before being committed to the special class, from 2 to 15 per cent of these children are each year successfully returned to the regular grades. However, after the child's physical defects have as far as possible been corrected and his health improved, if she then finds that under the most skillful instruction of which she is capable, he does not make progress sufficient to justify the slightest hope of his being able to compete successfully in the regular grades with pupils of approximately the same chronological age, she should then consider what can be done in the special class to prepare him for life upon leaving school. He has demonstrated his incapacity to achieve under the most favorable conditions and for him the special class becomes a finishing school.

There has been much time, money, and effort wasted in the education of subnormal children through failure to recognize clearly the proper aim of education in the case of this type of child. Since about 20 per cent of the adult population are engaged in unskilled labor the folly of attempting to prepare children of the most inferior intelligence for skilled labor or for clerical work is self-evident. The aim of the teacher, after a thorough trial in the special class has demonstrated the impossibility of the pupil's ever successfully doing regular grade work, should be to prepare him to become a law-abiding, self supporting citizen in the simplest occupations. The great need for special training is shown by the fact that the chances of subnormal pupils developing into delinquent adults are many times as great as is true of normal children. This does not mean that mental incapacity as such leads to delinquency but rather that these handicapped boys and girls have not been given the right kind of training and instruction. Under proper training a large percentage of them develop into law-abiding, self-supporting citizens. Fernald, the head of one of our well-known institutions for the feebleminded, has said that some of the most beautiful characters he has ever known were feebleminded boys and girls who had been properly trained.

In the education of the subnormal child the emphasis should be placed primarily on physical and manual training and the formation of desirable habits, and only secondarily on the acquisition of knowledge.

Good health and physical strength are of vital importance to the subnormal child since he is destined to earn his living by the use of his muscles. Without a healthy body under control he is doomed to become a public charge. Contrary to common belief he is apt to be handicapped physically as well as mentally, although not to the same degree. The manual activities which form such an important part of his training are to give him muscular coordination, to train the mind and the body to act together so that he may compete successfully in the simplest walks of life with individuals of normal mentality.

The formation of desirable habits in the education of the subnormal is no less important than the development of strength and skill, for, granting that he has acquired the strength and skill necessary to engage in unskilled labor, still he could not hold a job unless he went to work regularly day after day, got there on time, followed instructions, and kept out of trouble with his fellow workers. These habits, which are fundamental to success in any occupation, are the very ones that are essential to success in school work, although this point frequently has not been recognized by the teacher of the subnormal pupil. She has failed to realize that the child who is irregular in attendance, or comes late to school, or fails to pay attention when given instructions, or is constantly in trouble with his fellow pupils is slowly but surely forming habits which if persisted in, no matter how successful he may be in other respects, will prevent him from ever becoming a law-abiding, self-supporting member of society. Through the formation of right habits he may be led to do what is right and kept from doing what is wrong without understanding why some things are right and other things are wrong.

The emphasis placed on habit formation does not mean that the subnormal child is to be given no instruction in the traditional school subjects, but rather it means that his saturation point is less quickly reached in the domain of habit than in the realm of understanding.

It is desirable that more attention be given to the development of correct speech in subnormal children than is usually done. At best they will do little reading and still less writing, but speech is in constant demand, and the ability to express their ideas in simple grammatical language will be of the greatest value to them all through life in making social adjustments.

The subnormal child should, if possible, be taught to read, even if it means no more than the ability to read simple signs, such as *in, out, push, pull, stop, go, come in, keep out,* etc. Even this simple reading ability will be of value to him in his daily life both as a child and as an adult. The subnormals of more capacity should be taught to read, among other things, the daily newspaper, for this is what they will read after leaving school if they read at all.

Every subnormal child can be taught to write at least his own name, and many of these children can be taught to express their ideas in simple written language. They should be taught how to write the simple business and friendship letters that they will have occasion to write after leaving school. It is important, however, that in all their writing legibility, not speed, be emphasized, for the subnormal adult will have little occasion for letter writing.

In arithmetic it is a case of teaching the simple number combinations that the subnormal will have occasion to use in daily life outside of the school, and his greatest use of these combinations will be in connection with the making of change. If he has not been taught to make change quickly as well as accurately he will soon cease to count his change at the time of making a purchase. It is not so difficult to teach subnormal children the fundamental operations, addition, subtraction, multiplication, and division as it is to teach them when they should add, subtract, multiply, or divide. All formal number drill not accompanied by concrete problems is worse than useless.

In other words, to be successful in the education of subnormal children in our public schools it is necessary to break away from the traditional course of study in respect to subject-matter and methods of instruction. It is not a question of preparing these children for the high school but for life; the special class becomes a finishing school and the responsibility is placed fairly and squarely on their teacher to give them the type of training that will enable them as far as possible to become law-abiding, self-supporting citizens.

In one or more cities the plan is being tried of allowing some of the subnormal boys and girls between fourteen and sixteen years of age to work part-time under the supervision of the school. The aim is to give them a chance to show what they can do on a real job before it is too late to correct defects in their training. Many of them find their own jobs, while others are assisted by the school. In some cases they work only an hour or two each day and attend school the rest of the time; again they work a half day and attend school a half day; and in still other cases they are allowed to work full time for a period of several weeks. In all cases they are supervised by a teacher or someone appointed for that purpose, and when one fails to make good he is returned to the school full time for corrective training. By this plan it is believed that the course of training and instruction of these pupils can be improved to such an extent that a much larger percentage of them will become wholly or in part self-supporting.

The teacher required for subnormal children is one who has had successful teaching experience in the elementary grades; who has been trained in the giving of educational and psychological tests; and who has a thorough knowledge of the methods and subject-matter of instruction best suited to the subnormal child, as well as a good understanding of the nature and characteristics of backward and subnormal children. This means that part of the special teacher's training should include experience with children in an institution for the feeble-minded as well as with those in public school classes for the backward and subnormal. This kind of training is of value to the teacher in helping her to distinguish between the feebleminded who are emotionally stable and those who are unstable. The latter is the institutional type, for the cases belonging to this type generally prove to be least amenable to training and instruction and the greatest menace to society. Since at present it is impossible, even if desirable, to segregate all the feebleminded into our state institutions, it is of vital importance that we detect and segregate those who are most likely to become a social menace. There is no agency so well adapted to the detection of this type of child as the special class taught by a well trained teacher.

B. The Backward

While it is generally conceded that about 2 per cent of the school children are so retarded mentally that they should be educated in special classes, there is less agreement in regard to the number of backward children or so-called problem cases that stand in need of special education. Since most of these children have an intelligence quotient between seventy-five and ninety the difficulty is not poor intelligence alone but that accompanied by conditions which tend to keep achievement below the level of intelligence.

Some school systems have no special classes for the backward children as such but attempt to provide for them in the regular grades either by means of coaching teachers, or by grouping all pupils according to intelligence or achievement, each group advancing at its own rate. But in many school systems the backward children are simply allowed to fail and repeat the work with indifferent success until they reach the age when they can leave school, which opportunity most of them take advantage of to their own good.

In Grand Rapids the number of pupils in special classes for backward children is equal to 3.4 per cent of the enrollment in the first eight grades. The corresponding figure for Detroit is merely a fraction of one per cent, as Detroit is attempting to care for most of these pupils in the Z group of the regular grades, while Grand Rapids is making provision for them by means of special classes and coaching teachers. Whether it is best to provide for the backward pupils by means of special classes, coaching teachers, better classification in the regular grades, or by a

38

combination of these methods, may be a debatable question, but that these children constitute a real problem is scarcely open to debate as long as almost ten per cent of the pupils in the elementary schools are repeating the work they are taking.

Where special classes are provided for backward children the course of study usually does not differ in any marked way from that of the regular grades except that more emphasis is placed on minimum essentials. For generally the aim of these classes is not to provide a special education for backward pupils but rather to assist them to return to and make good in the regular grades. The class generally consists of from twenty to twenty-five pupils. The teachers of these classes frequently have had no special training for this work except that they have shown in the regular grades aptitude for and interest in handling difficult cases.

Where separate special classes for backward and subnormal children are found in the same school system, frequently the doubtful cases are tried out in the classes for the backward before being committed to the classes for the subnormal. But in some cities the classes for the backward are only for the older children who are not making good in the regular grades. Where there are no separate classes for delinquents they are usually found in the classes for the backward as it is generally easier to get them into these classes than into those for the subnormal.

C. The Subnormal and the Backward in Small School Systems

While much has been accomplished in the large cities in providing suitable training and instruction for backward and subnormal children, comparatively little has been done in the smaller cities and towns and in the rural districts. In these smaller school districts one course of study taught by the conventional methods has usually been offered to all with the result that those of inferior endowment have in no wise received the training and instruction suited to their needs. However, the large city seems to have certain marked advantages over the smaller communities when it comes to providing special education for the handicapped. Among these are greater wealth available for education, better facilities for psychological and medical examination of school children, more homogeneous grouping made possible by large numbers, and less interference from the parents.

However, most of the advantages of the large city are more apparent than real. The total cost of education in any community is increased only to a slight extent by the proper education of backward and subnormal children. Furthermore, without special education more of them become a burden to society, so that in the long run special education is cheaper than the present inefficient method of training these children.

39

It is necessary that large school systems have a more thorough and complete system of selecting pupils for special classes, since mistakes are not so easily corrected as in the smaller communities. The greater interest of the parent in educational problems in the smaller community makes it easier to enlist his sympathy and support for any measure that is educationally sound and means a better opportunity for his child.

It is true that it is not possible to have the variety of special classes in the small school district that may be found in many of the large cities. Neither is it possible in the small school system for the regular grade teacher to have as homogeneous a group of pupils to instruct nor as narrow a range of subject-matter to teach as in the large school system. This does not necessarily mean that her work is less efficient, but rather that her problem is different. Likewise, the problem of special education in the smaller communities is different from that in the large cities.

Special education in most large cities began with the "ungraded room" which served as a dumping ground for all kinds of misfits, the disciplinary cases predominating. The primary purpose of this room was not to provide a better opportunity for the problem cases but rather to relieve the regular grades of their presence. As a result of this policy these rooms were generally placed in the basement and taught by teachers better known for brawn than brains. This is still the case in some school systems. Under such circumstances the parents were inclined to think, and not without reason, that their child had gone from bad to worse when put into the ungraded room. The result is that today the ungraded room does not have a very savory reputation. To enter this room is commonly regarded as a punishment, not as a privilege. Consequently any school system that is starting special education and does not have enough backward, subnormal, and disciplinary cases for more than one teacher would do well to avoid the term "ungraded room". It is much better to call it the "opportunity room", for the primary purpose in establishing such a room should be to give the handicapped child a better opportunity of securing the training and instruction suited to his needs; not to relieve the regular grades of his presence, desirable as that may be.

The room selected for the opportunity class should be as well located, as attractive, and as well equipped as the other classrooms. It is hard to get parents and pupils to believe in the opportunity class if it is located in an unattractive poorly lighted basement room, and supplied with cast-off books and materials from the regular grades.

If we include under the head of problem cases, the backward, the subnormal, and the delinquent as well as pupils of defective speech, every school system with as many as three or four hundred pupils in the elementary grades doubtless has enough problem cases for one opportunity room. The number of backward, subnormal, and delinquent pupils in the public schools of Grand Rapids who are in special classes or schools is equal to 6.4 per cent of the total enrollment in the eight grades and this does not include the speech correction cases. It would seem then that 5 per cent would be a conservative estimate of the number of pupils in the elementary schools that stand in need of special education.

In the small school system where the special teacher has different types of problem cases under her instruction it is not necessary that all these pupils sit in the opportunity room. The children of defective speech could be sent to her for their lessons in speech correction; some of the backward children as well could sit in the regular grades and report to her for help. In some small places the special class teacher also assists pupils of normal intelligence who because of illness or other reasons have fallen behind in their work. Under this plan the door of the opportunity room swings both ways. It is easy to get in and just as easy to get out.

Some object to having the backward, subnormal, and delinquent children all in the same room on the grounds that each of these types needs to be handled in a different way. The answer is that the special teacher can meet these conditions more successfully than the regular grade teachers who have had no special training for teaching any of these types.

Again it is said that in the small school system the special teacher means the expense of one more teacher to handle the same number of children. It need not always mean this if the principal or superintendent will make the most of the possibilities of classification in the regular grades. It is related that one superintendent of a small school system started a special class by relieving the regular grade teachers of their most difficult cases on condition that for every problem case taken out of their rooms they accept five normal pupils in return. The result was a special class with a waiting list without increase in the number of teachers employed.

Some teachers are more successful in handling large groups of pupils well graded than much smaller groups representing a wide range in capacity and achievement. Why not make use of this fact at the time of the formation of the special class? A principal who has five teachers in the elementary grades should not plan to have the same number of pupils per teacher, but rather attempt to classify pupils in such a way that the teachers capable of handling large homogeneous groups will have the opportunity. We are rapidly approaching the time when every elementary school will have a specialist on individual differences, a teacher trained to handle problem cases. It is neither necessary nor desirable that every elementary teacher should spend the time, money, and effort required to prepare to teach exceptional children, for many teachers by nature are not qualified for this work; but it is essential that we have in every school system, large or small, at least one person

41

qualified by temperament, training, and experience to handle the problem cases that are found in every elementary school and which so long have been neglected.

It is desirable to avoid publicity in the organization and administration of the opportunity room. If simply known by parents and pupils as the room to which children, bright or dull, are sent who need special help, it becomes a very effective agency in improving conditions in the school, in that it renders efficient individual assistance where such assistance is needed and at the same time arouses in all teachers a greater interest in the individual child.

In selecting children for the opportunity room, it is well to make use of the age-grade distribution, intelligence tests, and the judgment of the teacher to insure that no pupils in need of special help are overlooked. Particular attention should be given to the children in the first grade, since so much more can be accomplished for those who have not become discouraged through repeated failure.

In a school system where there are only two or three small elementary schools, it may prove advantageous to transfer all problem cases to the school in which the opportunity room is located whether they sit in the opportunity room or not. This would obviate the necessity of any pupil's attracting attention by periodically going to another school for special instruction.

Let the opportunity teacher find out as much about each child as may be necessary for success in corrective work. In some cases much information will be needed; in others, very little. If expert psychological and medical examinations are not needed for diagnosis and treatment, it is better to dispense with them. Why waste time and effort in the accumulation of data not necessary for the successful treatment of the case? In all cases the use of the terms, "feeble-minded", "mentally defective", "moron", "imbecile", idiot", and "incorrigible" should be avoided. It is not the function of the opportunity teacher to make any such classification.

In the larger school systems where there are enough problem cases for two or more special teachers, it is generally wise to develop two types of classes: the special class for subnormals, those with an intelligence quotient below seventy-five who have failed signally to make good in the regular grades; and the opportunity class for all other problem cases. The class for the subnormals which has already been discussed is usually called the "special class". The name "subnormal" should be avoided for obvious reasons.

But what can be done for the problem cases in the rural schools? The situation cannot be adequately met until the consolidated school has become the rule instead of the exception, for, unfortunately, few rural teachers have had any training for teaching the exceptional child and many of them inadequate training for teaching the typical child. Yet much can be done for the rural teachers in service through wise supervision, extension courses, and summer schools, and those preparing to teach in the rural schools should be required to take one course dealing with the problem of special education.

In every community there are one or more problem cases who do not respond to training and instruction either in the regular grades or in the special class and who are trouble makers in both the school and the community. These are the cases that should be given a thorough medical and psychological examination, but unfortunately the smaller communities do not have adequate facilities for such examinations. A travelling psycho-medical clinic maintained by the state could render a real service to the smaller communities by the careful examination of all such serious problem cases and by making specific recommendations in regard to treatment or disposition. Through the influence of such a clinic many of these problem cases would be given adequate corrective training in the local community and many others would be committed to our state institutions (Appendix D) before they had entered upon a possible career of crime.

SELECTED REFERENCES

Anderson, Meta L., *Education of Defectives in the Public Schools.* The World Book Company, Yonkers on Hudson, New York, 1917

Goddard, H. H., *Feeblemindedness: Its Causes and Consequences.* The Macmillan Company, New York, 1914

Hollingworth, Leta S., *The Psychology of Subnormal Children.* The Macmillan Company, New York, 1920

Horn, J. H., *The Education of Exceptional Children.* The Century Company, New York, 1924

Huey, E. B., *Backward and Feebleminded Children.* Warwick and York, Inc., Baltimore, 1912

Tredgold, A. F., *Mental Deficiency.* William Wood and Company, New York, 1908

Wallin, J. E. W., *The Education of Handicapped Children.* Houghton Mifflin Company, Chicago, 1924

VI. THE TRAINING OF TEACHERS

In order to meet the demand for more and better trained teachers of handicapped children, the preparation of teachers for this work has been centralized at the Michigan State Normal College at Ypsilanti. Not only are special courses offered during the year as indicated below, but in the summer school as well.

If a superintendent who wishes to start a special class for mentally retarded children or for children of defective speech cannot secure a well trained teacher, he would do well to select one of his successful grade teachers fitted by temperament and interest for this work and have her take the summer school course. She could then organize the special class in the fall and continue her training either in extension courses or in summer schools. However, in the formation of a special class for the blind, deaf, or crippled where state aid may be obtained if certain conditions are complied with, the superintendent should be sure that the teacher selected meets the requirements of the state law. Information on this point can be secured from the state superintendent of public instruction. A liberal interpretation of the law is to be expected until well trained teachers are available.

While superintendents of schools can do much to advance the cause of special education for handicapped children by directing the attention of their grade teachers to the importance of this work, and by encouraging those who have the natural qualifications to specialize in this field, they can do much more by establishing special classes in their own school systems as soon as possible.

The general plan for the training of teachers of the deaf and hard of hearing, the blind and partially sighted, the backward and mentally defective, and the crippled, at the Michigan State Normal College, is clearly described in the following announcement prepared by Professor C. M. Elliott, Director of Special Education.

Requirements for Admission

"The laws providing state aid for the education of special types of children require that teachers of such children have special training and experience. In compliance with the legal conditions the State Board of Education adopted the following resolution:

"That hereafter no person shall be deemed qualified to teach any of the above-mentioned special types of children who shall not have had

- a. at least one year of successful teaching experience with normal children
- b. a state life certificate or its equivalent (two years) in college training
- c. one year of special technical training, in the field elected, in addition to the two years mentioned in (b)

Affiliations and Distribution of the Work

"In order to give the students of the department a thorough acquaintance with their problems, the work of the year of special training is distributed as follows:

"(a) One term of twelve weeks in residence at the Michigan State Normal College. This term is devoted to a study of the history and literature, and theoretical courses pertaining to the special field of teaching elected by the student.

"(b) One term of twelve weeks in residence at the state institution caring for the particular class of children the student is preparing to teach; thus those preparing to teach the deaf and hard of hearing spend the second term at the Michigan School for the Deaf at Flint; those preparing to teach the blind and partially sighted, at the Michigan School for the Blind at Lansing; those preparing to teach the subnormal, at the Michigan Home and Training School at Lapeer; and those preparing to teach crippled children at the Hospital School at the University of Michigan Hospital at Ann Arbor.

"During this term the student will be given an opportunity to study the several types of handicapped children in large groups, to get a thorough insight into the problems of their care in institutions and to pursue certain technical courses that can be given here to better advantage than elsewhere.

"(c) One term of twelve weeks at selected public school centers. Arrangements have already been made by which the public school systems of Detroit and Grand Rapids are open to our students for training purposes. This period of actual apprenticeship in public day-schools of first rank, gives the student a contact with the problem of special education in its various aspects that can be gotten in no other way. The above named cities have well-organized special departments and a full complement of special schools and classes, all of which are available for observation and practice.

Plan of Work and Credit

"Although the work of this year is distributed as described above, it must not be supposed that it is unorganized or indefinite. Each curriculum consists of carefully planned courses bearing directly upon the work the student is undertaking, and having a definite sequence. Four units of college work will be covered each term, and the student satisfactorily completing the work will be entitled to one year of college credit, which may be applied upon the requirements for the degree of Bachelor of Science granted by the Normal College.

"As the courses offered at the several locations are repeated each term, students may enter at the beginning of any regular college term."*

There is no state in the Union that has in operation a more comprehensive plan for the training of special teachers than the one outlined above.

APPENDIX A

An Act to authorize the board of education of any school district to establish and maintain day schools or classes for those who are blind or have defective vision, and day schools or classes for those who are deaf or have defective hearing, to provide for the expense of the same, to provide for the supervision of such schools or classes, and other help to carry out the provisions of this act, and to repeal act number two hundred twenty-four of the public acts of nineteen hundred five and all acts amendatory thereto.

(Act 122, P. A. 1923)

The People of the State of Michigan enact:

Section 1. The board of education of any school district may, upon a petition of parents or guardians of five or more resident children between the ages of three and twenty years who by reason of being blind or having defective vision, or who by reason of being deaf or having defective hearing, cannot profitably or safely be educated with the other classes in the public schools of such district, establish and maintain within the limits of the district one or more day schools or classes for the instruction of such children. In all cases the blind and deaf shall be given separate instruction. The instruction of the deaf shall be by the "oral" method. Such special schools or classes shall be placed in rooms properly equipped for such special classes and shall be maintained so long as there shall be an actual attendance of not less than five children who are blind or have defective vision or five children who are deaf or have defective hearing, if the parents or guardians of such children are legal residents of this state. Such necessary equipment shall comprise the books, appliances, and apparatus necessary for the instruction of such children.

Sec. 2. Courses of study, adequacy of methods of instruction, qualifications of teachers, the conditions under which teachers are employed, and the necessary equipment and any special services for such children

---

*For further information in regard to course of study, write to Professor C. M. Elliott, Director of Special Education, State Normal College, Ypsilanti, Michigan.

46

for any school year must comply with the requirements prescribed by the superintendent of public instruction. Teachers shall be employed in the same manner as other public school teachers of the district are employed. All persons appointed to teach in any such schools or classes for the deaf shall have had special training for such teaching, shall have had at least one year's experience as a teacher in a school for the deaf, and shall be graduates of a training school for teachers of the deaf by the "oral" method.

Sec. 3. The board of education of any district which maintains one or more such schools or classes shall make an annual report to the superintendent of public instruction or oftener if he shall so direct, which report shall include an itemized statement of all expenditures for said schools or classes, including the salaries of teachers, special equipment, special material, together with such other facts relative to such schools or classes as the superintendent of public instruction may deem necessary for the proper administration of this act.

Sec. 4. The board of education of a school district where one or more such schools or classes are established shall include in its annual budget a sufficient sum to provide special service for said pupils and to maintain said schools or classes and out of said sum it shall pay said teacher or teachers monthly. To reimburse said city or district for such expenditure, the state treasurer is hereby authorized to pay to the treasurer of the proper school district, out of the general fund of the state, on or before July first in each year, upon the warrant of the auditor general, the actual expense incurred for teachers' salaries, for the purchase of the necessary special school equipment and for any special services required for such schools or classes, which shall have been conducted in accordance with this act during the same number of months of school as is prescribed for the school district for other classes, as shown by vouchers filed with the auditor general and certified to be correct by the superintendent of public instruction. The total amount per pupil paid to any one school district for the purpose herein provided shall not exceed the difference between the average per capita cost of instruction and equipment for the other children in the first eight grades of said school district and the average per capita cost required to pay teachers' wages and the cost of the necessary special school equipment to educate the children enrolled in the classes established for those children who may be included within the provisions of this act. In no case shall the amount paid exceed two hundred dollars for each child instructed in said school district during the school year, and a part of such sum proportionate to the time of instruction of any pupil so instructed less than the number of months prescribed for the school district for the year. The board of education of any school district that does not maintain a class for the children named in this act may pay the tuition of any such children to a school maintaining such schools or classes.

SEC. 5. The board of education maintaining one or more such schools or classes shall cause to be executed monthly, vouchers in triplicate upon forms prepared and furnished by the auditor general so as to show the rate of salary paid to instructors of such schools or classes and the time covered by such payment; also vouchers in triplicate upon forms prepared and furnished by the auditor general showing the special school appliances purchased and the price paid for each article or series of articles. The treasurer of said school district is required to forward two copies of these receipted vouchers to the superintendent of public instruction within the first five days of the month succeeding the month covered by the payment. On or before the fifteenth day of each month the superintendent of public instruction shall present one set thereof to the auditor general, authorizing him to pay to the treasurer of the proper school district the amount covered by the certified vouchers presented.

SEC. 6. The superintendent of public instruction shall have general supervision over work done under this act. Expenses of such supervision subject to the general supervisory control of the state administrative board, shall not exceed twenty-five hundred dollars in any one year and shall be paid from the general fund of the state in the same manner as other state expenses are paid.

Sec. 7 repeals act 224 of 1905.

APPENDIX B

An Act to authorize the board of education of any school district to establish and maintain schools or classes for those who are crippled, to provide for the expense of the same, to provide for the supervision of such schools or classes, and other help to carry out the provisions of this act.

(Act 313, P. A. 1923)

The People of the State of Michigan enact:

SECTION 1. The board of education of any school district may, upon a petition of parents or guardians of five or more resident children between the ages of six and twenty years who, by reason of being crippled, cannot profitably or safely be educated with the other classes in the public schools of such district, establish and maintain within the limits of the district, one or more schools or classes for the instruction of such children. In all cases the crippled shall be given separate instruction. Such special schools or classes shall be placed in rooms properly equipped for such special classes and shall be maintained so long as there shall be an actual attendance of not less than five children who are crippled, if the parents or guardians of such children are legal residents of this state. Such necessary equipment shall comprise the books, appliances, and apparatus necessary for the instruction of such children.

SEC. 2. Courses of study, adequacy of methods of instruction, qualifications of teachers, the conditions under which teachers are employed, and the necessary equipment and any special services for such children for any school year must comply with the requirements prescribed by the superintendent of public instruction. Teachers shall be employed in the same manner as other public school teachers of the district are employed. All persons appointed to teach in any such schools or classes for the crippled shall have had special training for such teaching.

SEC. 3. The board of education of any district which maintains one or more such schools or classes shall make an annual report to the superintendent of public instruction or oftener if he shall so direct, which report shall include an itemized statement of all expenditures for said schools or classes, including the salaries of teachers, special equipment, special material, together with such other facts relative to such schools or classes as the superintendent of public instruction may deem necessary for the proper administration of this act.

SEC. 4. The board of education of a school district where one or more such schools or classes are established shall include in its annual budget a sufficient sum to provide special service for said pupils and to maintain said schools or classes and out of said sum it shall pay said teacher or teachers monthly. To reimburse said city or district for such expenditure, the state treasurer is hereby authorized to pay to the treasurer of the proper school district, out of the general fund of the state, on or before July first in each year, upon the warrant of the auditor general, the actual expense incurred for teachers' salaries, for the purchase of the necessary special school equipment and for any special services required for such schools or classes, which shall have been conducted in accordance with this act during the same number of months of school as is prescribed for the school district for other classes, as shown by vouchers filed with the auditor general and certified to be correct by the superintendent of public instruction. The total amount per pupil paid to any one school district for the purpose herein provided shall not exceed the difference between the average per capita cost of instruction and equipment for the other children in the first eight grades of said school district and the average per capita cost required to pay teachers' wages and the cost of the necessary special school equipment to educate the children enrolled in the classes established for those children who may be included within the provisions of this act. In no case shall the amount paid exceed two hundred dollars for each child instructed in said school district during the school year, and a part of such sum proportionate to the time of instruction of any pupil so instructed less than the number of months prescribed for the school district for the year. The board of education of any school district that does not maintain a class for the children named in this act may pay the tuition of any such children to a school maintaining such schools or classes.

SEC. 5. The board of education maintaining one or more such schools or classes shall cause to be executed monthly, vouchers in triplicate upon forms prepared and furnished by the auditor general so as to show the rate of salary paid to instructors of such schools or classes and the time covered by such payment; also, vouchers in triplicate upon forms prepared and furnished by the auditor general showing the special school appliances purchased and the price paid for each article or series of articles. The treasurer of said school district is required to forward two copies of these receipted vouchers to the superintendent of public instruction within the first five days of the month succeeding the month covered by the payment. On or before the fifteenth day of each month the superintendent of public instruction shall present one set thereof to the auditor general, authorizing him to pay to the treasurer of the proper school district the amount covered by the certified vouchers presented.

APPENDIX C

An Act to Provide Free Treatment for Children, whose Parents or Guardians are Unable to Pay

Act No. 274 of the Public Acts of 1913, which takes effect August 14, 1913

House Enrolled Act No. 136

An Act to provide for the medical and surgical treatment of children who are afflicted with a curable malady or deformity, and whose parents are unable to provide proper treatment, providing for the expenses thereof, and prescribing the jurisdiction of the probate court in such cases.

The People of the State of Michigan enact:

SECTION 1. Whenever any agent of the board of corrections and charities, supervisor, superintendent of the poor, or physician, shall find within his county any child who is deformed or afflicted with a malady which can be remedied, and whose parents or guardians are unable to *provide proper care and treatment,* it shall be the duty of such agent, supervisor, superintendent of the poor, or physician, to make a report of such condition to the probate judge of the county in which such child resides. Upon the filing of such report with the judge of probate it shall be his duty to cause a thorough investigation to be made through the county agent, or a superintendent of the poor, and a physician appointed by him for that purpose.

SEC. 2. If upon investigation the judge of probate is satisfied that the parents or guardians are unable to provide proper medical or surgical treatment, and the physician appointed to make the examination shall certify that, in his opinion, the deformity or malady is of such a nature that it can be remedied, the judge of probate may enter an order directing that said child be conveyed to the University hospital at Ann Arbor for free treatment to be paid for by the State as hereinafter provided: Provided, That no such child shall be sent to or received into said hospital unless in the judgment of the physician in charge thereof, there is a reasonable chance for him to be benefited by the proposed medical or surgical treatment, and for this purpose a complete history of the case shall be furnished by the examining physician.

SEC. 3. It shall be the duty of the superintendent of the University of Michigan hospital, upon receiving such child, to provide for such child a cot or bed or room in the University hospital, and he shall also assign or designate the clinic of the University hospital to which the patient shall be assigned for the treatment of the deformity or malady in each particular case, the care and treatment of such child, and the physician or surgeon in charge shall proceed with all proper speed to perform such operation and bestow such treatment upon such child as in his judgment shall be proper.

SEC. 4. No compensation shall be charged or allowed to the admitting physician of said hospital, or to the physician or surgeon or nurse who shall treat said child, other than the salary respectively received from the board of regents of the University of Michigan.

SEC. 5. The superintendent of the University hospital shall keep a correct account of the medicine, nursing, food and necessities furnished to said child, and shall make and file with the auditor general, an affidavit containing an itemized statement as far as possible of the expenses incurred at said hospital in the treatment, nursing and care of said child in accordance with the rates fixed by the regents.

SEC. 6. Upon filing said affidavit with the auditor general, it shall be the duty of said auditor general forthwith to draw an order on the treasurer of the State of Michigan for the amount of such expenditure, and forward the same to the treasurer of the University of Michigan. It shall be the duty of the auditor general upon receipt thereof to credit the amount thereof to the University of Michigan, in accordance with his warrant drawn by him for the University hospital.

Sec. 7. The county agent or superintendent of the poor shall receive the sum of three dollars a day, except in counties where such officer or officers shall receive a fixed salary and his actual expenses while making the investigation herein provided, upon the order of the judge of probate. All claims of the county agent or superintendent of the poor for making the investigations, and actual traveling expenses and a fee of five dollars for the physician for making the examination upon the order of the probate judge under the provisions of this act, and all expenses incurred in conveying such children to and from the University hospital shall, when approved by the judge of probate ordering such services, be audited by the auditor general and paid out of the general fund. The expenses of sending such children home may be paid by the hospital and charged in the regular bill for maintenance in the discretion of the superintendent of the hospital when he is satisfied that the parents or guardians are unable to bear such necessary expense.

APPENDIX D

Public Acts, 1923—No. 151

An Act to revise and consolidate the laws organizing hospitals for the insane, homes and schools for the feebleminded and epileptic, institutions for the discovery and treatment of mental disorders; to regulate and provide for the care, management and use thereof; to provide for the licensing, visitation and supervision of privately owned hospitals, homes and institutions for the care and treatment of such mentally defective persons; to provide for the apprehension of persons believed to be insane, feeble-minded, mentally defective or epileptic, and their commitment, to provide for their care, custody, parole and discharge, to provide penalties and to repeal certain acts or parts of acts contrary to the provisions hereof.

The People of the State of Michigan enact:

Section 11. The father, mother, husband, wife, brother, sister, child, or guardian of a person alleged to be insane, feeble-minded or epileptic, or the sheriff or any superintendent of the poor, or supervisor of any township, or county agent, or any peace officer within the county in which such alleged mentally diseased person resides, or may be, may petition the probate court of said county for an order directing the admission of said person to a hospital, home or institution for the care of the insane, feeble-minded or epileptic, such petition to contain a statement of the facts upon which the allegation of such mental disease is based and because of which the application for the order is made. Upon receiving such petition the court shall fix a day for hearing thereof and shall appoint two reputable physicians to make the required examination of such alleged mentally diseased person; such physicians shall file their report duly certified to with the court on or before such hearing. Notice of such petition, and of the time and place of hearing thereon, shall be served personally, at least twenty-four hours before the hearing, upon the person alleged to be so mentally diseased, and any sheriff, officer, or county agent who made the petition, father, mother, husband, wife, or some one next of kin, of full age, of such alleged mentally diseased person, if there be any such known to be residing within the county, and upon such of said relatives residing outside of the county and within this state as may be ordered by the court, and also upon the person with whom such alleged mentally diseased person may reside, or at whose house such person may be. This notice may be served in any part of the state. The court to whom the petition is presented may dispense with such personal service or may direct substituted service to be made upon some person to be designated by it. The court shall state in a certificate to be attached to the petition its reason for dispensing with personal service of such notice, and, if substituted service is directed, the name of the person to be served therewith. In such cases the court shall appoint a guardian ad litem to represent such mentally diseased person upon such hearing, and in other cases it may appoint such guardian ad litem. The court shall also institute an inquest, and take proofs, as to the alleged insanity, feeblemindedness, epilepsy or mental disease of such person, and fully investigate the facts before making such order, and, if no jury is required, the probate court shall determine the question of such alleged mental disease of such person. If the court shall deem it necessary, or if such alleged mentally diseased person, or any relative, or any person with whom he may reside, or at whose house he may be, shall so demand, a jury of six freeholders having the qualifications required of jurors in courts of record, shall be summoned to determine the question of insanity, feeblemindedness or epilepsy, and whenever a jury is required the court shall proceed to the selection of such jury in the same manner as is provided for the selection of a jury for the condemnation of land for railroad purposes, and such jury shall determine the question of insanity, feeblemindedness, epilepsy or mental disease of the alleged mentally diseased person. The jurors shall receive the same fees for attendance and mileage as are allowed by law to jurors in the circuit court. Pending such proceedings for admission into the proper home, hospital or institution, if it shall appear, upon the certificate of two legally qualified physicians, to be necessary and essential so to do, the court may order such alleged mentally diseased person to be placed in the custody of some suitable person, or to be removed to any hospital, home or retreat, to be detained until such petition can be heard and determined: Provided, however, That the period of such temporary detention shall not exceed thirty days, unless the court shall, by special order, enlarge the time. Such alleged mentally diseased person shall have the right to be present at such hearing, unless it shall be made to appear to the court, either by the certificate of the medical superintendent in charge of such hospital, home or retreat to which he may have been temporarily admitted, or by the certificate of two reputable physicians, that his condition is such as to render his removal for that purpose, or his appearing at such hearing improper and unsafe. If such person shall be found and adjudged to be insane, feebleminded, epileptic or mentally diseased, the court shall immediately issue an order for his admission to the proper hospital, home or institution for his care and treatment. In case the admission of such mentally diseased person is ordered as a public patient, then the county of which such person is a resident shall be liable to the state for the support of such patient for one year. If the relative or friends of such mentally diseased person shall so request, or if on investigation at the time of commitment it shall appear that such mentally diseased person has means or property sufficient for the payment of his care or maintenance, or if those persons legally liable for the care and maintenance of such mentally diseased person have sufficient means for that purpose, the court shall order his admission as a private patient, to any hospital, home or institution for the care or treatment of the insane, feebleminded or epileptic in this state, and shall specify the amount in the commitment that the estate of such mentally diseased person, or those persons personally liable for the care and maintenance of such mentally diseased person shall pay for care and maintenance of such mentally diseased person in such state institution, and the amount so stated shall be subject to collection the same as any other moneys due the state are collected.

SEC. 12. The court may appoint a proper person or persons to take such mentally diseased person to the hospital, institution, home or retreat, who shall each receive as pay for such services the sum of three dollars a day, together with his necessary expenses. The court, upon making such order for admission into such institution, if, in his judgment, a guardian of such mentally diseased person is needed before a guardian of his or her person and estate can be regularly appointed, may, by a separate order and without further notice, appoint summarily a guardian of the person only of such mentally diseased person, which guardianship of the person shall continue only until a guardian both of his person and estate shall be regularly appointed. Such guardian of the person shall give a bond in such sum as may be directed by the court, and with sureties to be approved by the court. The guardian shall have the same rights and be subject to the same duties with respect to the person of his ward as guardians of incompetent or insane persons have by law, except that he shall not interfere with the admission and detention of such mentally diseased person pursuant to the order for admission.

SEC. 13. The order for admission shall be substantially in the following form:

State of Michigan,

The probate court of the county of.....................At a session of said court, held at the probate office in the .... of .... in said county, on the .... day of ...., A. D.....

Present Hon. .... Judge of Probate.

In the matter of .... (insane, feebleminded or epileptic).

...............................having been appointed for hearing the petition of ....:..... praying that said ....be admitted to the .... as a patient, and due notice of the hearing on said petition having been given as required by law and as directed by said court, the said petitioner appeared ....

. It appearing to the court upon filing the certificates of two legally qualified physicians, and after a full investigation of said matter, with .... the verdict of a jury that said .... is ....: (insane, feebleminded or epileptic) and a fit person for care and treatment in said institution and that .... should be admitted to said institution as a patient.

It is ordered, that said .... be admitted to said institution as a .... patient.

It is further ordered, that .... be and is hereby authorized and directed to remove said .... to said institution, with full power and authority for that purpose.

....
Judge of Probate

SEC. 14. After said order for admission has been regularly made and entered as provided herein, the judge of probate shall mail a certified copy of such order to the medical superintendent of the institution to which the patient has been committed, and upon receipt of such order the said medical superintendent shall, as soon as there is room for such patient at such institution, notify the judge of probate of that fact, whereupon the judge of probate shall cause the patient to be transported to said institution for admission thereto: Provided, That no person shall be admitted to any such instituton under such order after the expiration of twenty days from and including the date of receipt of such notice by the judge of probate.

Sec. 15. The state shall pay all the expense incurred by any of such state institutions in the care, maintenance, custody and treatment of any feebleminded, insane, epileptic or mentally diseased person committed to any institution named in section one of this act except as herein otherwise provided.

Lightning Source UK Ltd.
Milton Keynes UK
UKHW022117081218
333475UK00006B/142/P